Stations
of the Cross
for the Elderly

Fr. Christopher Rengers, O.F.M. Cap.

Our Sunday Visitor Publishing Division
Our Sunday Visitor, Inc.
Huntington, Indiana 46750

INTRODUCTION

There is a tradition that the Blessed Virgin herself would visit and walk again the sorrowful path that marked the last steps of her Son. From early on, pilgrims visited the Holy Land to reflect on the life of Jesus. Later, the Crusaders, largely unsuccessful in military efforts, brought back strong impressions of the original Way of the Cross. So the custom gradually grew of  putting up visual representations of the scenes along the Way.

The number of stops, or stations, varied from five to thirty or even more. It was not until 1731 that Pope Clement XII set the number at fourteen. In the meantime, the devotion of St. Francis of Assisi to the Passion of Christ, and the work of the Franciscans who had charge of the shrines in the Holy Land, helped to make the devotion popular. St. Leonard of Port Maurice, especially, preached the Way of the Cross and set up and blessed hundreds of Stations in churches during forty years of popular mission preaching. The privilege of blessing Stations of the Cross was reserved to Franciscans until recent times.

Among my cherished memories is the devotion of my Dad to the Stations of the Cross. One of his customs was to pray the Stations in any church or chapel he visited for the first time. Another custom was to pray the Stations after Mass as the final part of thanksgiving after Holy Communion. As a boy, more ready for the walk home and breakfast, I felt the minutes expanding into seeming hours in those days of fasting from midnight before receiving Holy Communion.

"If anyone would be my disciple," Jesus said, "let him take up his cross daily and follow after Me." We often ask ourselves: "Why must I suffer? Why is there much suffering in the world? Why did Jesus, the God-man, have to suffer?" Making the Way of the Cross helps us to know the deeper answers, and to have a more complete understanding of our own Way of the Cross.

The Stations of the Cross may be made without moving from station to station. During Lent, a priest and servers move from station to station. The congregation stays where it is in the pews.

The Stations of the Cross can become a companion to the Rosary, and can also be made at home, using a booklet such as this one. (When the feet cannot move well, the eyes can yet travel from station to station.) In fact, a set of the Stations can be displayed around the walls of a room in the home or erected in the backyard.

One idea not usually mentioned concerns St. Joseph. Mary and her dying Son must have missed him. Since Jesus gave His mother to the care of St. John, we presume that St. Joseph had died earlier. A practice that can help "put St. Joseph on Calvary" is to invoke him or pray his litany between the hours of noon and 3:00 p.m.

St. Joseph had walked with Jesus along many a path, but he did not have the blessing to walk near Our Lord on those last steps of ordinary earthly life. Yet his example and manly training had helped to form the courage that Jesus needed for His last painful journey, carrying the cross.

We do well to ask St. Joseph to help the elderly and all who walk a personal way of sickness and sorrow to find the courage to walk bravely and to embrace the cross. He can also give all of us the unspoken assurance: Jesus loves me.

FR. CHRISTOPHER RENGERS, O.F.M. CAP.

Jesus Is Condemned

V. We adore You, O Christ, and we praise You.

R. Because by Your holy cross You have redeemed the world.

Jesus speaks: A pagan judge, Pontius Pilate, sees through the deceits of My accusers, My own countrymen, over whom I wept. In an effort to save Me, he has Me scourged. The Roman soldiers then add to this by mocking Me and crowning Me with thorns. But Pilate's words, "Behold the man," which are aimed at stirring up pity, only stir up renewed cries of "Crucify Him! Crucify Him!" So, out of weakness, fearing for his own political skin, he condemns Me to death by crucifixion.

I respond: Sometimes, Jesus, when I hope for pity or at least consideration, I am passed by in silence, which tells me the other person is not interested. Sometimes I am reproved instead, even mocked for clumsiness or lack of comprehension. Words float back to me, snatches of conversation I'm not supposed to hear. They cut like scourges. My head may throb in frustration, recalling Your crown of thorns.

Of course, sometimes my own exaggerated feelings invite such humbling hurt. Help me, Jesus, to remember You, condemned to death, yet most innocent of all wrong and good to all. In my heart, may the hope of Pontius Pilate when he said, "Behold the man," come true. May it be a heart turned in pity and sympathy toward You.

Lord Jesus Crucified, have mercy on us.

Jesus Takes Up the Cross

V. We adore You, O Christ, and we praise You.

R. Because by Your holy cross You have redeemed the world.

Jesus speaks: I have been looking forward to My final hours. Yes, I have been looking not only with longing but also with sadness and dread. In the prime of My vigorous manhood, the Father is calling for Me to give up life. My human nature, complete like yours, feels the sadness and dread of approaching death. I know ahead of time the sufferings and the manner of death. The prophecies and the hearts of My enemies tell Me.

My prayer to always do the will of the Father makes Me more certain of the Father's plan. It has to clearly represent the most complete giving so that all can understand the completeness of My love for them and the justice and mercy of the Father. The thought of it in the garden made Me sweat blood. Now the crossbeam is laid on My shoulders. The final hours are here.

I respond: Lord Jesus, in my later years the thought of approaching death comes more often. For me, it brings a combination of longing and sadness and dread. I long to see You face-to-face, to meet our Mother Mary and her loving husband, Your virgin-father, Joseph. My spiritual reading and the Church's liturgy have made me a friend of many saints. I look forward to meeting them. Many relatives and friends have gone before. My guardian angel is waiting.

But the barrier of death is a blind barrier. Faith tells me of the unknown on the other side. But the thick, dark side here looms before my earthly eyes. Then, too, this world is beautiful with its changing seasons, its flowers, its sunrises, and its sunsets. There are good friends here, too, and dear relatives. I ask, Lord Jesus, to embrace my final cross, signifying death, with courage, to meet it with open eyes, and to accept it and offer it as joined to Your cross, as the plan of the Father for me.

Lord Jesus Crucified, have mercy on us.

Jesus Falls

V. We adore You, O Christ, and we praise You.

R. Because by Your holy cross You have redeemed the world.

Jesus speaks: In the garden of My agony, when the soldiers seized Me, I said, "This is your hour, and the power of darkness." I also reminded Peter, who drew his sword, that I could ask the Father to send legions of angels to defend Me.

But for now, the plan of the Father calls on Me to rely only on My ordinary human abilities. And these, just like yours, are subject to loss of blood, to fatigue, to the emotions. So it is, that soon after taking up the cross I fall, much to the merriment of some bystanders. Laughter and uproarious shouts of amusement ring in My ears.

No angels come to help, for the Father does not will them to come. But the angels, you can be sure, are not far away. I lie in the dust, as the words of the psalm describe Me: "I am a worm and no man."

I respond: I understand, dear Jesus, how You feel, for it happens more often now that I am old, that some bodily or mental weakness makes me do or say things that cause embarrassment. It is not a fall to the ground, of course, but a fall from the image of strength and sureness that I like my friends and companions to see. Help me to accept facts and not hide in some imagined cocoon that is transparent to others. Instead, let me learn to have that transparency of simplicity that befits a humble soul. May my guardian angel help me from putting on a false front.

Lord Jesus Crucified, have mercy on us.

THE FOURTH STATION

Jesus Meets His Mother

V. We adore You, O Christ, and we praise You.

R. Because by Your holy cross You have redeemed the world.

Jesus speaks: Five days ago, a woman watched people wave palm branches, sing out their "Hosanna" welcome, and spread garments before Me. She stood along the way, hoping, praying, that somehow, as in the case of Abraham and Isaac, the Father would not demand the supreme sacrifice of her Son's life.

Yes, it was My own dear mother who watched on Palm Sunday. Now she stands again and watches the waving palm of yesterday replaced by the menacing fist of today. We don't need to speak to each other. She looks at Me. I look at her. The story is complete. She knows this has to be the last chapter.

I respond: Lord, thank You for giving me this glimpse into the sorrowful heart of Your mother, more sorrowful than others because it is immaculate. The heart completely untainted by sin can love You in the most complete way. But untainted hearts — or purified hearts — can also enter more deeply into the pain of Your Most Sacred Heart. Their love is the measure of their sorrow.

A person like Your mother does not need to wail and weep aloud or exclaim. One tear glistening on her cheek proclaims the silent profusion of the tears of her sorrow for You, and of her forgiving love for me and for everyone. Help me to know that one touch on the shoulder, one compassionate glance, or a written note from a relative or friend often tells me more than a torrent of words.

Lord Jesus Crucified, have mercy on us.

Simon of Cyrene Helps Jesus

V. **We adore You, O Christ, and we praise You.**

R. **Because by Your holy cross You have redeemed the world.**

Jesus speaks: The Father knows everything. Take this meeting along the way to Calvary. Simon of Cyrene has come to Jerusalem for the great holy days of the Passover. He is one of many thousands gathered in the Holy City. To the soldiers who grab him and force him to help Me, he is just one of a milling, jostling crowd. He looks strong. To My Father, he is a man chosen to be at this spot at this time. (Has My mother, in her quiet way, helped?) To the eyes of the crowd, and in the laughter of some, he is the unlucky one. But you know he is the chosen one. That is why you know his name today.

I respond: Yes, Lord Jesus, I understand that what the majority of people think little of is often great in the eyes of God. Those who laugh at Simon or count themselves happy not to be in his place are the less-favored ones. I'm sure that some people account me ill-favored. They notice my halting words as I struggle to remember. They see my stiff way of walking. They see the sick and the old not able to walk. Some are confined to a wheelchair; some to a bed.

Yet, in the gracious plan of the Father, as St. Francis de Sales said, God has seen this moment from eternity. Help me to recognize the moments of grace in my life, and to say, "Thanks be to God," whether the moment is one of joy or sorrow, one of acceptance or rejection by the crowd, just one moment, or one of a long string of painful moments. May my every moment be a Simon-moment, helping You to carry the cross of salvation.

Lord Jesus Crucified, have mercy on us.

THE SIXTH STATION

Veronica Wipes Jesus' Face

V. We adore You, O Christ, and we praise You.

R. Because by Your holy cross You have redeemed the world.

Jesus speaks: Veronica represents many good women who did acts of kindness for Me. Her name means "true image." She also represents many good women who do acts of kindness to others for love of Me. As long as you do something for the least of My brothers in My name, you do it for Me. In each case, My image is impressed on the heart of the one who helps the cause of justice or does the work of charity.

I respond: Yes, Lord, I understand that in all persons who have a need, whether for food or drink, for clothing, for consolation, or for any of the spiritual and corporal works of mercy, I should see You. They are all struggling on their Way of the Cross. Every true act of love for the least one, done for You, will leave an impression on my heart. I also know that this works likewise for those who aid me in sickness or in the weakness of old age.

So then, teach me to accept help in this way when I need it. The help given me in Your name can also impress Your image on the hearts of my helpers. Whether I help or am helped, my heart can always grow lighter as I understand this truth.

Lord Jesus Crucified, have mercy on us.

Jesus Falls Again

V. We adore You, O Christ, and we praise You.

R. Because by Your holy cross You have redeemed the world.

Jesus speaks: There is a sharper interior pain when, after being helped, you find yourself again helpless. My mother, Mary, and Simon and Veronica have just provided Me, in different ways, with a new courage. Now My mother's face has faded into the nameless and blurred faces of the crowd, among them those taunting Me with their lips curled, and the Veronicas pressing the veils of past memories to their hearts. Simon helps carry the *patibulum* (crossbar), but My feet still refuse to carry Me.

Now I stumble, and My face lies in the well-trodden dust of Jerusalem. This brings renewed, sharp pain from the crown of thorns. But the sharper pain comes from the thought of falling just after being helped.

I respond: Lord Jesus, I know how this is. Kind relatives and friends come to comfort me, to try to raise my spirits, to take my mind from the aches of the body, to pass an hour with me on the back porch of stored memories. Then before long, some new demand of the body intrudes. Some rude reminder jumps at me from the lips of a tired, overworked nurse. Some new doubt comes to cast a blurring shadow across my conscience. After being helped, I'm again helpless. There is nobody who could be expected to understand. Show me, then, Jesus, how to get up again and go on. You promised that Your yoke would be easy and Your burden light.

Lord Jesus Crucified, have mercy on us.

Jesus Meets the Women of Jerusalem

V. We adore You, O Christ, and we praise You.

R. Because by Your holy cross You have redeemed the world.

Jesus speaks: "Daughters of Jerusalem, do not weep for Me; weep rather for yourselves and for your children. For the days will surely come when people will say, 'Happy are those who are barren, the wombs that have never borne, the breasts that have never nursed.'"

These are the words I speak to the weeping women who stand along the way, their frightened children clinging to them. I am not refusing their tears, but remembering the tears I Myself have shed over Jerusalem. How often My heart has yearned for that city, so rich in the history of My people, made holy by its Temple, enshrining the memories of so many of My Father's great servants.

The yearning of My heart meets only the pride of those hearts turned against the truth. The shaft of truth's arrow cannot pierce the armor of pride, sin, and blind preconception. I do not refuse tears, but look beyond to the tears of these clinging children in their adult years. Not a stone will be left upon a stone. There will be none to dry the tears of their children.

I respond: Yes, Lord, there are tears along the way to the Hill of the Skull. The pity that Pontius Pilate tried to arouse when he presented You to the crowd brought not tears but jeers and renewed shouts of "Crucify Him!" Pilate's efforts were further rebuffed by Your enemies' choice of the criminal Barabbas over You, the man of perfect innocence. Here on the cheeks of weeping women is the answer Pilate sought in vain. In their hearts is the answer.

Help me, Lord, as I grow old, not to grow in hardness of heart, refusing to drop an ancient grudge, refusing to forgive the injury I still remember even as I become more forgetful of other things. This puts me in the company of those who chose Barabbas. Help me, rather, to join the holy women who wept over You.

Lord Jesus Crucified, have mercy on us.

Jesus Falls a Third Time

V. We adore You, O Christ, and we praise You.

R. Because by Your holy cross You have redeemed the world.

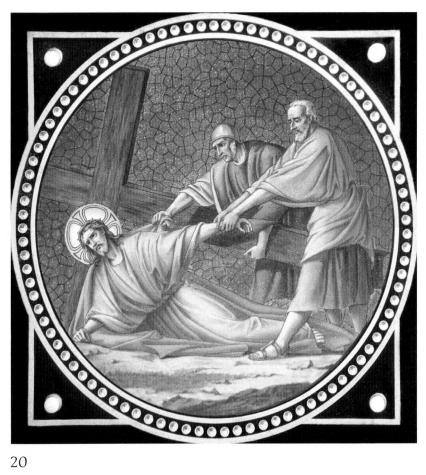

Jesus speaks: There is a strong contrast between a person standing and a person fallen or lying on the ground. There is also a big difference between one who walks with confidence and ease and one who stumbles and sways. People ask, "What is the trouble?" Good people gather around the fallen person and try to help.

As I lie in the dust of the city street, no one rushes to help. Rather, the soldiers prod Me. Do you notice the contrast between the Man in the dust and the Man who walked on the water of the Sea of Galilee, and the contrast between the groans of the fallen Man and the confident voice that rebuked the winds and the sea and made them calm? My helplessness is measured against the former show of strength and power. My helplessness now is the proof of how much I long to help all men reach heaven.

I respond: Yes, Lord, I know that You took on the fullness of my weak human nature. You experienced everything except sin. I want to join You in accepting the weakness more often felt with advancing age, the greater dependence on others' help. I remember the scampering of my youth, and the sometimes-proud stride of maturity. My gait now is uncertain, sometimes stumbling. I could fall and break bones. Help me to offer my dependence on others, my helplessness joined to Yours, as the force behind my hope and longing to help others reach heaven.

Lord Jesus Crucified, have mercy on us.

Jesus Is Stripped

V. We adore You, O Christ, and we praise You.

R. Because by Your holy cross You have redeemed the world.

Jesus speaks: At the beginning of My life, My mother wrapped Me in swaddling clothes. That was not far from here, a few miles away at Bethlehem. Her hands had the careful, gentle touch of all young mothers. She brought with her the recent skill of helping her cousin Elizabeth with the infant John. Now the soldiers pull away My garments. They cast lots for the seamless one. The scourging has left My body a mass of wounds. Now the rivulets of blood flow again.

There is new pain. There is worse pain — from embarrassment. I offer everything to My Father. I recall the words of Job: "Naked came I out of my mother's womb, and naked shall I return thither." My mother recalls the swaddling clothes, the many garments that through the years her hands have made for Me and for Joseph, who was given to be My father on earth by My Father in heaven.

I respond: Lord, sometimes in sickness or old age I go back to the dependency of infancy. I need help in clothing myself, in divesting. It certainly affords a great time for exercising humility, for realizing how caring even for the very simple needs of life can be beyond me. So, especially in these times, I offer the pain of dependency to atone for sins against modesty, my own and others'. I also ask Your blessing on those suffering from cold because they lack suitable lodging and clothes.

Lord Jesus Crucified, have mercy on us.

Jesus Is Crucified

V. We adore You, O Christ, and we praise You.

R. Because by Your holy cross You have redeemed the world.

Jesus speaks: The good people who have walked with Me on the Way of the Cross have counted three falls. Now there can be no more, for My feet are nailed to the cross. A long spike has torn through flesh. It has separated and scraped bones. My ordinary earthly journeys are ended. My feet can no longer bear Me to the desert to enjoy its quiet and solitude in prayer to My Father. They cannot carry Me to the Temple or to the homes of My friends; neither can they take me to fishing boats nor bear Me to the gathering places where in the open air I proclaimed the Kingdom. My hands, pierced at the wrists, cause Me more pain than the feet, for here the big nails rub against a large nerve center.

But each shooting pain is an arrow that wings its message of utmost love, even to those who have nailed shut the doors of their hearts.

I respond: Lord, I thank You for explaining Your sufferings. Sometimes the pains of advancing years make a person fretful. The pain echoes in the violence of my speech. Help my relatives and friends and nurses to hear more the message of discouragement and pain than the exact meaning of the words that burst from my lips. Help me to remember Your silence before Your judges, to recall Your words turned not to accuse or shout, but rather telling in renewed prayer to Your Father that Your heart is not nailed but free and gentle. I echo Your words: Father, forgive them, for they do not know what they are doing.

Lord Jesus Crucified, have mercy on us.

Jesus Dies

V. We adore You, O Christ, and we praise You.

R. Because by Your holy cross You have redeemed the world.

Jesus speaks: One day a young man asked Me what to do to reach the kingdom of heaven. We counted up the commandments of God, and he said: "All these I have kept." But he turned away from my invitation: "If you would be perfect, go sell all you have and give to the poor and then come, follow Me."

On the cross, My words to John and to My mother have bespoken the fullness of that poverty. The last wrench of My heart has broken the bond of filial possession by this visible giving of My own mother to the beloved disciple. I have forgiven those who have hurt Me most, then I have promised heaven to the thief on my right. There remains only to feel even the separation from My Father in heaven. "My God, my God, why hast Thou forsaken Me?" My full thirst to please Him and save souls is complete, My will to live has run its course, and I, at last, can cry from the cross: "Father, into Thy hands I commend My spirit. It is finished."

I respond: Yes, Lord, I see now that the way of poverty is the way to perfection. It is not just the poverty of not having money or home. It is the poverty of losing the strength of the body, and sometimes the clarity of the mind. It is the giving up of the final clinging to a grudge, to ill will, resentment, and self-pity. The poverty ensuring perfection may mean accepting the neglect of friends and family, of being forgotten.

Complete poverty is giving up life at the end of my earthly pilgrimage. Help me to embrace a new generosity daily, saying, "I thirst for fulfilling the Father's plan. I thirst for souls." Finally, with restful joy, help me to say, "Father, into Thy hands I commend my spirit" and to hear from You: "Come, you blessed of my Father, you have walked the way of His plan for you. You have finished His work."

Lord Jesus Crucified, have mercy on us.

Jesus Is Taken From the Cross

V. We adore You, O Christ, and we praise You.

R. Because by Your holy cross You have redeemed the world.

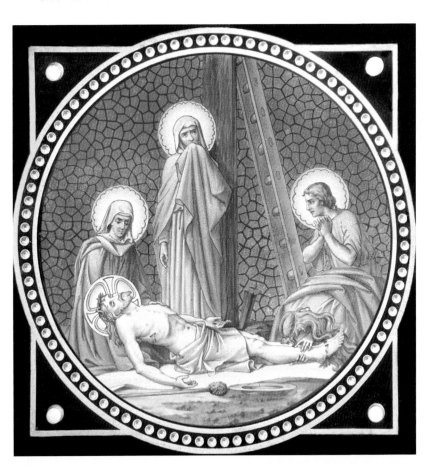

Jesus speaks: My mother was not able to comfort Me as all good mothers would do, by soothing My brow, by clasping My hands. They were nailed above, and My head was covered by the crown of thorns. She had held Me as an infant, and had kissed away the pains of tumbling boyhood's scratches and bruises. Now she again holds My body, a mass of bruises, cuts, wounds. She is the first of all to enter into the union of suffering with Me for the redemption of men. As my apostle Paul wrote in his letter to the Colossians, "I now rejoice in my sufferings for you, and fill up those things that are wanting of the sufferings of Christ, in my flesh, for His body which is the Church."

Nothing is wanting in a bare, absolute sense, but My Father's plan extends to others the gift of joining in My redemptive suffering. Wasted pain is a great loss because there need be no wasted pain if those who have faith in Me will only exercise that part of the faith that invites them to be joined with Me in My redemptive suffering.

I respond: Yes, Lord, I understand pain only when I understand that it is conscious redemptive suffering, or when it is a preparation for such union with Your cross. I am grateful to Christian artists for giving me touching paintings and statues of Your mother holding Your body just taken from the cross. Help me to be stirred not only to natural pity, but more to fruitful imitation of Your mother and my mother, in suffering with You for the salvation of souls. The assurance that pain need not be wasted, that it fulfills the plan of the Father, is comforting. This assurance is a great gift of advancing age, when discomfort and pain await my calm embrace. May Mary teach me her way.

Lord Jesus Crucified, have mercy on us.

Jesus Is Buried

V. We adore You, O Christ, and we praise You.

R. Because by Your holy cross You have redeemed the world.

Jesus speaks: Once my voice called out, "Lazarus, come forth," and My friend, four days in his tomb, rose from the dead. You can see now the completeness of the gift My Father asked of Me. The voice that calmed wind and sea, that called the dead back to life, that rebuked demons, is stilled in death. The hour of cruelty came, the forces of evil apparently triumphed, the earth trembled, and the mid-afternoon wore the black garments of night in mourning.

A friend, Joseph of Arimathea, arranged with Pontius Pilate for the burial. He gave his own tomb, hewn in the rock nearby. My disciples went into hiding; the violence had drained their courage. As the Father had asked the utmost of Me, so He asked the utmost of them in paying the price of dashed hopes and the coin of confusion about a trusted leader fallen. The shepherd has been struck, and the sheep have fled.

I respond: Yes, Lord, once You said the foxes have lairs and the birds of the air have nests, but the Son of Man has nowhere to lay His head. Death is Your final poverty, and its exterior wrapping is the tomb. But I know it is "only a borrowed tomb." I join in the sorrow of Your mother, Joseph of Arimathea, Mary Magdalene and John, and the women who laid Your body to a hasty rest. They will return to complete the burial with more care and cere- mony. But the tomb will be empty. I ask, Lord Jesus, as my time of death comes closer, to remember more often the day when my now-failing body will be restored to life and vigor, and I will join You in happy resurrection.

Lord Jesus Crucified, have mercy on us.

Prayer After the Stations

Dear Lord Jesus, I have walked with You along the Way of the Cross. I have stood with Mary at the foot of the cross. I have heard Your last words. They have opened Your heart for me. Just as the lance pierced Your heart, so my heart has also been pierced.

I mourn my sins and failings. Your pain and sorrow remind me of the price You paid for my sins and the sins of the world. But they also remind me of the depth of Your mercy. They remind me that You paid a great price. But You paid for a great prize, my salvation. Your open heart tells me that the gates of heaven were opened by Your sacrifice. I have seen the rock sealing the tomb. But I know that on the third day the rock was moved, and You came forth, the glorious victor over pain and death. The empty tomb and the words of the angels, "He is risen … He is not here," fill me with the hope that one day all tombs will be empty, that those who have joined You on the Way of the Cross will have a glorious resurrection.

Dear Lord Jesus, give me daily the peace You brought to all who saw You on the day You rose from the dead. Give me the hope that I will one day be forever happy with You in heaven, my true home. Amen.